JAZZIN ABOUT
STANDARDS

PIANO/KEYBOARD

PAM WEDGWOOD

FABER *ff* MUSIC

Contents

© 2010 by Faber Music Ltd
First published in 2010 by Faber Music Ltd
Bloomsbury House 74–77 Great Russell Street London WC1B 3DA
Music engraved by Jackie Leigh
Cover by Velladesign
Printed in England by Caligraving Ltd
All rights reserved

ISBN10: 0-571-53406-6
EAN13: 978-0-571-53406-7

To buy Faber Music publications or to find out about the full range of titles available
please contact your local music retailer or Faber Music sales enquiries:

Faber Music Limited, Burnt Mill, Elizabeth Way, Harlow, CM20 2HX England
Tel: +44 (0)1279 82 89 82   Fax: +44 (0)1279 82 89 83
sales@fabermusic.com   fabermusic.com

track 1

How High the Moon

Words by Nancy Hamilton
Music by Morgan Lewis

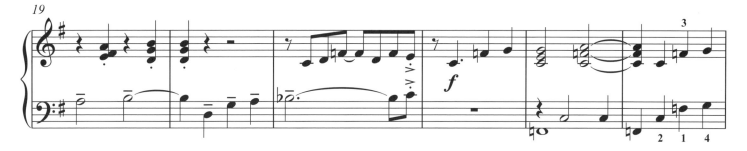

track 2

Have You Met Miss Jones?

Words by Lorenz Hart
Music by Richard Rodgers

track ③

Elite Syncopations

Scott Joplin

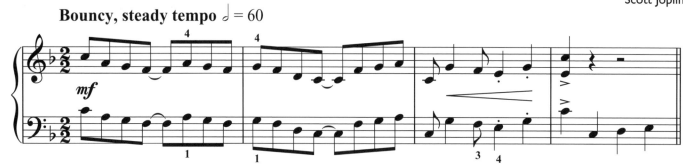

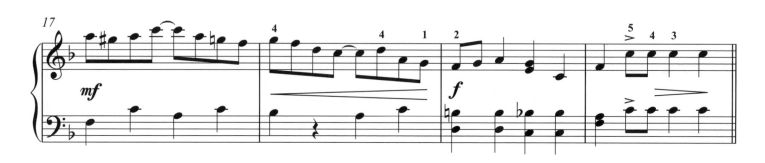

track 4

Night and Day

Words and Music by
Cole Porter

track 5

Embraceable You

Music and Lyrics by
George Gershwin and Ira Gershwin

track 6

Monty the Moocher

Pam Wedgwood

In swing tempo ♩ = 108

In prowling mode!

Stamp foot on
2nd and 3rd beats

Stamp foot on
2nd and 3rd beats

poco rit.

tr

Ped.

track 7

Good Morning Blues

Words by James Rushing
Music by Count Basie and Eddie Durham

track 8

High Pressure

Pam Wedgwood

With a strong beat ♩ = 126

track 9

The Days of Wine and Roses

Words by Johnny Mercer
Music by Henry Mancini

track 10

Blues in the Night

Words by Johnny Mercer
Music by Harold Arlen

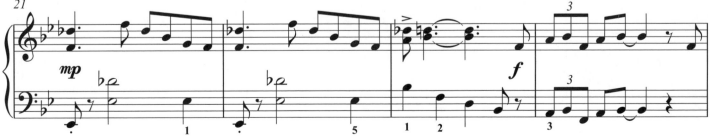

track 11

It Ain't Necessarily So

Music and Lyrics by George Gershwin, Du Bose
and Dorothy Heyward and Ira Gershwin

Relaxed swing ♩ = 88

AFTER HOURS

Alarm clocks, barking dogs, telephones, meetings and rush hour … the hustle and bustle of life. What better way to relax than to sit down at the piano, chill out and indulge yourself with music from Pam Wedgwood's *After Hours*?

With a variety of pieces in styles to suit any mood—sentimental ballads to cosy dinner jazz, wistful blues to cheerful, upbeat tunes—*After Hours* provides the perfect antidote to stress. So conjure up the dimly lit atmosphere of a jazz club, and relax with these lush harmonies and laid-back melodies …